A Little History of the Schulenburg Family

written for my newborn nephew
Theodore August Werner
(XXIV Generation, 2013-today)
by
Fritz Schulenburg-Beetzendorf
(XXIII Generation, 1985-today)

This 'short history' is not intended to show academic research results. All stories are based on information from written and published family histories, various online sources and stories gathered from family members and historians.

Washington DC
2014

Bibliografische Information der Deutschen Nationalbibliothek
Die Deutsche Nationalbibliothek verzeichnet diese Publikation in der Deutschen Nationalbibliografie; detaillierte bibliografische Daten sind im Internet über http://dnb.d-nb.de abrufbar.
1. Aufl. - Göttingen : Cuvillier, 2014

Nonnenstieg 8, 37075 Göttingen
Telefon: 0551-54724-0
Telefax: 0551-54724-21
www.cuvillier.de

1. Auflage, 2014
Gedruckt auf umweltfreundlichem, säurefreiem Papier aus nachhaltiger Forstwirtschaft.

ISBN 978-3-95404-748-2
eISBN 978-3-7369-4748-1

Special thanks to my mother Ines, my brother Daniel and his wife Clémence, my uncles Rudolf and Paul-Werner, my cousin Nicolas, Georgiana Cavendish, Anna Mautner Markhof, Morten Freidel and Peter Lang for helping me realize this story.

Foreword from the Head of the Schulenburg Family

On 28th of October 1237, the Margrave and the Bishop of Brandenburg signed a contract on the distribution of taxes ("the tithe") between the church and the Margrave's government. Eighteen witnesses from both sides signed the treaty, which can still be seen in the Museum of the Brandenburg Cathedral. One of the witnesses was the priest of Cöln, a village which later became part of Berlin. This is why Berlin claims to originate in 1237. Another witness was Wernerus de Sculenburch, who was a knight and the head of the administration of the Margrave's government; today this person would be called prime minister. Since Wernerus is the oldest proven ancestor of the Schulenburgs, the history of the family dates back to 1237 as well.

Since then the family has experienced good and bad times and the lives of the family members reflect their respective times. Today, 777 years later, the family consists of 70 male cousins and their family members. A family gathering takes place every second year. The 109th family gathering took place in September 2013 in Vienna which is where the famous Johann-Matthias Schulenburg met Prince Eugen roughly 300 years ago.

As the current Head of the Schulenburg Family, I would like to express my gratitude to Fritz, for writing the first history of the Schulenburg Family in English. His summary of the history of this family is well conceived and written and it is based on many documents, among them reams on the Schulenburgs that has been published over the past 120 years. None of this material has been published in English. With this book, Fritz portrays how our family members over the past 24 generations have managed their lives in both the good and tragic times of German and European history.

Graf Johann-Matthias von der Schulenburg (XXII Generation)

The Beginning – Origins of the Schulenburg Family in the Margraviate of Brandenburg (13th Century)

The Schulenburg family comes from a small barren region in Northern Germany named the Altmark. The Altmark (in English: *Old March*) is a region comprising the northern third of the State Sachsen-Anhalt. Today one can find small beautiful ancient towns in the area such as Salzwedel, Beetzendorf, Stendal, Tangermünde and Gardelegen. As the Altmark was the initial territory of the Brandenburg Margraves, it is sometimes referred to as the "Cradle of Prussia", as Otto von Bismarck was born close to the city Stendal.

The first Margrave (a German old title similar to Marques) of Brandenburg – the famous conqueror and war hero Albrecht the Bear – conquered the Altmark in the 12th Century and founded several villages. The Altmark received its name at the time of the rise of Albert in the region. A March – or Mark – referred to a border region similar to a frontier, comprising the border between two countries. As Albrecht´s land grew further to the East, a "Newmark" (New March) was founded and the remaining land became known as the "Alt (Old) mark". Often aristocratic families like the Schulenburgs were left in these regions and endowed with castles and land to start cultivating and organizing the lands connected to certain payments to the Margrave to finance further wars on the frontiers. Later in 1150, Albert the Bear made the fortress of "Brandenburg an der Havel" part of the Margraviate of Brandenburg[1]. It became the nucleus of the Margraviate.

With Albrecht the Bear, the Schulenburgs most likely entered the region even though their exact origin prior to the Altmark is unclear, since it was only in the 13th Century that people started carrying last names.

The first proven document clearly naming a Schulenburg that is in a line connected to the Schulenburgs living today dates back to 1237 when the Knight *Wernerus de Sculenburch* (II Generation of the Schulenburgs[2]) approved together with others in a contract a comparison of tax rights between the Margrave and the Bishop of Brandenburg.

---

[1] Today "Brandenburg an der Havel" is a small town compared to nearby Berlin, but it was the original nucleus of the former realms of Brandenburg and Prussia.

[2] The First Generation is covered by Conradus in 1187 – however, as the only written documentation of him is in a copy done in the 16th century which is not proven to be correct, historians do not consider him to be the first "Schulenburg" in the line. Additionally, one is not clear about the connection to Wernerus.

Picture 1: Margraviate (Mark) Brandenburg in 1320[3]

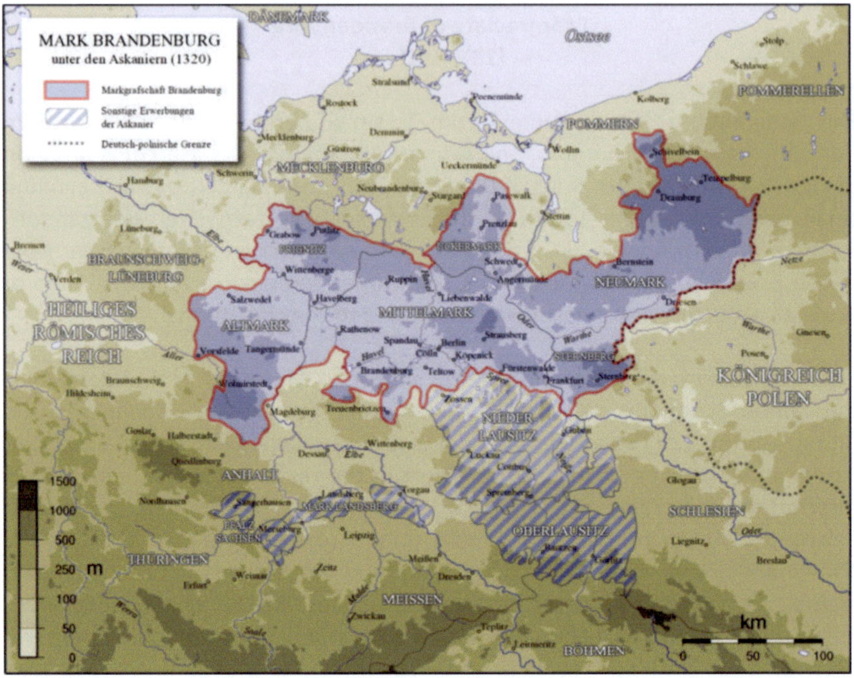

---

[3] Source: http://commons.wikimedia.org/wiki/File:MarkBrandenburg.png (25-Sep-2013).

Gaining Importance in the Margraviate of Brandenburg – Split into White and Black Line (14th Century)

Under the Margrave of Brandenburg, the Schulenburgs worked their way up by defending several castles and supporting the Margrave regionally. Additionally, as the Schulenburgs were hard-working and successful landlords, they contributed significant payments for the expansion towards the East. By the early 14th Century, the Schulenburgs owned several villages and manors in the region. Among them were villages like Audorf where a beautiful romanic church still stands from the 12th Century. Other smaller villages are located around Salzwedel, the second largest town in the Altmark. One of the first castles endowed to the Schulenburgs was a small castle close to Salzwedel, from which the name "Schulenburg" most likely comes ("Schulen" coming from "Schauen" (to look) and castle coming from a "Burg" (castle), from which you can look far). Today one can only see a few hills where this castle used to stand.

Picture 2: Romanic church in Audorf from approx. 1140[4]

[4] Photo was taken in 2013.

In the 14th Century the Schulenburgs included the town Beetzendorf in their belongings and with that the castle in Beetzendorf. From there until today Beetzendorf has been the "House" where all Schulenburg family branches originated from. In 1340 Bernhard I (IV Generation) and Dietrich II (IV Generation) – the two sons of Werner II (1271-1304, III Generation, endowed with the castle close to Salzwedel) – separated the ownership in Beetzendorf into two clearly separated tenure parts. This separation was the formal step of separating the Schulenburgs into two main lines – the "White" and the "Black Line" (Stamm).

The acquisition of the castle in Beetzendorf – where one can still see today a Romanic, nostalgic ruin – built a foundation for a long-lasting footprint in the region and for further expansion of the Schulenburgs in the Margraviate. As part of further expansion, the Black Line acquired Apenburg and also built a small castle in the Southern part of the town, which can still be seen today.

Picture 3: Old castle ruin in Beetzendorf today[5]

[5] Photo was taken in 2013.

Start of a Long Lasting Relationship with the Hohenzollern (14th and 15th Century)

During the subsequent centuries, the Wittelsbacher (todays "Bayern" family, 1323-1373) and the Luxemburgs (1373-1415) ruled over the Margraviate. Under the law named "Goldene Bulle" (1356) issued by Karl IV, the Margraviate was upgraded into an electing Dukedom "Kurfürstentum". This meant that the ruler of the region was entitled to elect, together with six other regions (the archbishops of Trier, Cologne and Mainz and the secular leaders of Bohemia (Böhmen), Palatine (Rhein) and Saxonia (Sachsen)[6]) throughout the Roman German Empire, the Roman-German King.

During these days of power struggles and battles in the Margraviate, the most important and influential member of the Schulenburg family was Dietrich III (V Generation). Dietrich was born in Beetzendorf as the youngest son of Bernhard I – the founder of the White Line. As often among important families in the Middle Ages, the youngest son was sent on a clerical path. Nevertheless, Dietrich, who was born around 1330, waited until he was nearly eighteen years old when he decided to actively pursue his parents´ wish. Dietrich first became canon (Domherr) and priest and later Provost. Later in 1365 he was elected as the first Bishop of Brandenburg (based in "Brandenburg an der Havel" where the diocese had been building a cathedral since the 10th Century). Dietrich was an influential politician and key advisor to Otto III ("the lazy one") of Brandenburg who came from the Wittelsbacher family and ruled until 1373. Dietrich advised him on strategies on how to remain Margrave and rule independently despite the increasing influence of King Karl IV. Additionally, Dietrich helped Otto raise funds for the region. When in 1373 Otto had to give his ruling rights back to the King, Dietrich lost a significant part of his power. Additionally, the Bishopric was struggling due to increasing dues and taxes from the Vatican (Pope Innocent VI and Urban V). Nevertheless, Dietrich was able to remain in place and became one of the advisors of Karl IV and his son. Dietrich was in close dialogue with the other Schulenburgs, providing them with an endowment for the villages Rohrberg (close to Beetzendorf and Groß Wismar) and Ladekath in 1383. Dietrich´s tombstone shows the family crest, the crest of the Bishopric, Dietrich holding a book, and the Bishop´s throne, and can still be seen today in the Dome of Brandenburg. Additionally, a metal plate on the altar of the dome refers to his death as the 33rd Bishop of the monastery.

---

[6] Later in the 17th Century Bayern and Brunswick-Lüneburg were added.

Picture 4: Tombstone of Dietrich III (V Generation) located in the Dome of Brandenburg an der Havel[7]

Emperor Karl IV placed his nephew – Jobst of Mähren – as Margrave of Brandenburg. As Jobst was not the strongest leader, the Luxemburgs slowly lost power in the region and the power of the regional aristocrats rose. One of the most interesting people living during those cruel and lawless times was Bernhard von der Schulenburg from the Black-Line (VI Generation, died in 1453). He was the owner of Beetzendorf, Apenburg and other estates. With the interest to increase his belongings, he pillaged several towns and fought against the City of Mecklenburg and the Archbishop of Mecklenburg. These times of outlaws made Bernhard become one of the most successful thieves and robber knights in the region.

While Bernhard was using the time of weak leadership in Brandenburg to pillage other villages, the Hohenzollern made an arrangement with the potential next King of Germany named Sigismund from the House of Luxemburg. They voted for Sigismund in 1410 to become King and were

[7] Source: Dietrich Werner Graf von der Schulenburg and Hans Wätjen, Geschichte des Geschlechts von der Schulenburg, p. 66.

therefore in return given power over the Margraviate of Brandenburg. This was the route of a long lasting reign of the Hohenzollern (today's "Preussen" family).

The Hohenzollerns´ family ruler Friedrich VI of Nürnberg became Margrave of Brandenburg (Friedrich I of Brandenburg). This brought new dynamics to the area. Several aristocratic families from the area who were involved in diverse conflicts and lootings in the region at first refused to support Friedrich. The two biggest rivals were the Putlitz and the Quitzow families. First, Bernhard also supported the Quitzows in their rebellion but soon changed his mind when he met Friedrich I of Brandenburg and realized he was a young, energetic Duke interested in gaining the local aristocrats´ support. Bernhard must have also figured that opposition against Friedrich would be a tough matter. As Friedrich I was trying to bring peace to the region, he caught Putlitz on one of his looting sprees and arrested him. The Quitzows´ castles and belongings were completely destroyed by Friedrich. As Friedrich – a good negotiator – had an interest in Quitzow´s skills and great relationship to other local aristocrats, Friedrich offered him freedom under the restriction that Quitzow would support Friedrich and support him in his duties. Friedrich´s plan succeeded and peace reigned in the Altmark and the Margraviate of Brandenburg again.

Even though Bernhard kept looting towns, he supported Friedrich with such efficiency against neighbouring states (e.g. the Dukedoms of Mecklenburg, Sachsen and Stettin) that Friedrich I knighted him in 1420 when the Brandenburg troops defeated against all odds[8] Otto of Stettin in Angermünden. Since Friedrich I and later his son, Friedrich II, highly respected Bernhard´s support, wise advice, and financial help[9], they made him as the first Schulenburg "Governor" (Landeshauptmann) of the Altmark. In the next generations this duty was often served by Schulenburgs. In 1416 Friedrich additionally granted him the ministry (Vogtei) in Salzwedel. During his days as a Governor, he was able to implement several peace treaties with his neighbours and was able to install rules, regulations, and normality. Meanwhile, Friedrich I established his residence in Berlin.

At the same time as Bernhard had these achievements, the White Line was financially successful mainly due to Busso I (VII Generation) and his sons. They were able to develop close relations with the Bishopric of Magdeburg (which the Schulenburg had fought a few years earlier), that enabled them to amass

[8] The ratio was most likely 1 to 4. Georg Schmidt, Das Geschlecht von der Schulenburg, Teil II, page 69.

[9] Bernhard had given Friedrich several loans throughout the years.

wealth. This laid the basis for several estate acquisitions in Brandenburg and other regions within Magdeburg such as Angern, Osterwohle, Brome, and Liebenburg close to Goslar.

Picture 5: Castle Angern[10]

By the end of Bernhard´s presence as a Governor, the Schulenburgs had increased their belongings to over 22 villages in the Altmark. Through these landholdings, along with the uprising of Friedrich I and the Hohenzollern, the Schulenburgs were able to become one of the most important families in the Margraviate.

[10] Source: Alexander Duncker, Sammlung Duncker Lithographien, 1857-1883.

Local Policy under the Hohenzollern and Wars with Pommern (Pommerania) (15th Century)

Under the Hohenzollern, Brandenburg became the leading power in Northern Germany, at the same time as the Schulenburgs started to expand their properties beyond the Altmark. The first signs of this expansion included the purchase of Angern (1448) and Altenhausen (1485) by the White Line. Meanwhile, the Black Line was also prolific and expanded by acquiring different parts throughout the Magraviate of Brandenburg, such as Erxleben or Klötze.

The outstanding figures representing this expansion phase among the Schulenburgs came mainly from the Black Line. A particularly impressive person of that time was Werner XI (VIII Generation, died 1515) whose bust was part of the Siegesallee-Tiergarten assemble (today it can be seen in the museum Zitadelle Spandau in Berlin-Spandau). Commissioned by Kaiser Wilhelm II in 1900, this bust together with others was produced by Otto Lessing and intended to honour the most influential Germans in history.

Werner XI supported Friedrich II and later Albrecht Achilles of Brandenburg in their wars against the neighbouring region of Pommern (Pommerania) in which Albrecht entitled Werner XI to the Commander of the newly conquered cities Gartz and Oder. Werner was one of the key drivers of the peace treaty of Prenzlau. The so called "Prenzlauer Frieden" was a compilation of several treaties during the series of wars between the Margraviate of Brandenburg and the Duchy of Pommern fought for control of Pommern-Stettin, and possession of the Uckermark. After the second treaty Albrecht endowed Werner with the castle Löcknitz for his great successes.

In 1477 Gartz and parts of the country including Löcknitz were reconquered by the Pommerns and Werner was taken hostage. In the following year, Albrecht of Brandenburg retaliated and was able to regain most essential access paths and streets that led to Stettin and various other cities that were important to retain the infrastructure of the land (e.g. Löcknitz, Vierraden). As a consequence, Albrecht forced the Pommern Duke to a peace treaty. Nevertheless, Gartz remained part of Pommern. Due to Werner´s charm and understanding of the interests of leaders during these days, Werner was able as a hostage to gain the Pommern´s Duke Bogislaw´s trust. Bogislaw was so impressed that he made Werner the Governor of Stettin and gave him the castle and city of Penkun. Herewith, Werner held the highest rank in Pommern below the Duke. This trust by Bogislaw was also significantly supported by the fact that Bogislaw had married a daughter of the Brandenburg Duke in 1477.

Picture 6: Werner XI von der Schulenburg (VIII Generation, +1515)[11]

Werner v. d. Schulenburg.

At the same time, the Margrave Johann (brother of Albrecht and head of Brandenburg) named him “Hofmeister“. With the trust of both leading figures of Pommern and Brandenburg, Werner contributed to the peace between the two states for many years. Together with Chancellor Jürgen Kleist, Werner worked on several reforms in the country, which makes Bogislaw X one of the greatest leaders Pommern ever had. They implemented a new financial and law system, stopped the ongoing lootings, increased trade and traffic, and established peace in the land. Even when the Duke of Pommern started his pilgrimage to Palestine in 1496, Werner managed the country alongside “von Kleist”. Until Werner passed away in 1515, he was active as a diplomat for many different countries. His sons inherited several properties and manors.

[11] Georg Schmidt, Das Geschlecht von der Schulenburg, Teil II, page 112.

Schulenburgs during and post Reformation (16th Century)

Shortly after Werner XI died, reformation ideals in Germany developed (approximately 1517-1521) when Martin Luther expressed doubts over the legitimacy of indulgences and the "plenitudo potestatis" of the Catholic Church and the Pope. With the 95 Theses written by Martin Luther, which were mainly against Catholic clerical abuses, especially the sale of indulgences,[12] and the subsequent excommunication of Martin Luther in 1521, the "Protestant Reformation" in Northern Germany and in Brandenburg began.

Before continuing to discuss Werner´s son Richard II (IX Generation, died 1536), two interesting much younger nephews of Werner from the White Line should be mentioned in this context – Christoph and Fritz.

Christoph V (XI Generation, died in 1580) was an impressive person living his life close to decision makers of the Reformation. He studied in 1530 in "Frankfurt an der Oder" and after five years, became catholic head priest of the monastery in Diesdorf. Later in 1547 Christoph was asked to become head priest (Propst) in Ratzeburg and was unanimously elected a few years later as Ratzeburg´s catholic bishop. The protestant patron of Ratzeburg – Duke Franz I of Sachsen-Lauenburg – had hoped that his son Magnus II would be elected and that he could in this way convert the diocese to Protestantism. When the Duke was disappointed by the outcome of the election, he and his alliances conquered the bishopric. Christoph was able to flee and only returned once the villains had left. Christoph figured that it was difficult to keep a catholic bishopric in a protestant surrounding. After negotiations with the Duke of Mecklenburg, Christoph received an indemnity payment and resigned from his position. He was the last catholic bishop in Ratzeburg. Later in his life he converted officially to Protestantism and married Anna von Estorf who gave birth to Albrecht (XII Generation, 1557-1607) who is the ancestor of almost all Schulenburgs living today. Therefore, people nowadays sometimes say that all Schulenburgs can be traced back to a Catholic bishop.

Christoph´s brother Fritz VIII (XI Generation, died in 1589) lived more the life of a mercenary independent of any confession and supported the Catholic Emperor Karl V and the Duke of Brandenburg in different battles. With great successes, Fritz VIII was able to gain significant landmarks throughout Northern Germany and among them Hehlen in 1560. His wife Ilse von Saldern – after a painful divorce – built in the region near Hameln and the river Weser the

[12] Martin Luther nailed the theses onto the Castle Church doors in Wittenberg (in Sachsen).

beautiful Renaissance castle Hehlen, which was one of the most impressive castles of its kind in that region. An impressive monument in remembrance of Fritz VIII can still be seen in the courtyard of the castle today.

Picture 7: Weser[13] Renaissance Castle Hehlen

Christoph and Fritz are examples of the turmoil and change that the region underwent from Catholicism to Protestanism, which is in line with the change of the Schulenburg family more generally. Other Schulenburgs were more convinced by the new school of thought. Matthias III (XI Generation, White Line), for example, who lived in the castle of Altenhausen was so impressed by Martin Luther when he met him in Wittenberg, that he asked a Lutheran priest from Wittenberg – despite a clear prohibition of protestant thoughts in the region by the Archbishop of Magdeburg – to come to Altenhausen and to join as a priest.

Independent of religious convictions, the political implication of the Reformation and secularization in Brandenburg (post 1535) offered several opportunities to increase the Schulenburg estates and to acquire new estates. Monasteries and other religious lands were taken by the Duke and afterwards given to diverse aristocrats. In most of these cases the White Line and the

[13] A river close to the city Hameln.

Black Line operated together and tried to gain the responsibility and "tenure" of these newly Margrave-owned estates. Examples include the acquisition of the monastery Dambeck or monastery Horst.

Returning to Werner XI and his sons, as Werner XI had not only a successful career as an officer but also as a politician and negotiator, the generations after him benefited from his material fortune and success. Werner´s son Richard II (IX Generation) acquired large estates such as Lieberose and was also able to further increase the wealth of the family.

Picture 8: Postcard from the beginning of the 20th century of castle Lieberose[14]

When his youngest son, Joachim II (X Generation), inherited his father´s and his grandfather´s (Werner XI) estates and later his cousin's Georg V estates as he had no male successors, Joachim was considered to be the richest man[15] in Northern Germany. His register named his belongings on 205 pages in 25 different cities and villages. "Joachim the Rich" as they called him, was a very religious, protestant, intellectual and generous person, in contact and a friend with the leaders of many different countries. He was in close dialogue with Duke Albrecht of Prussia, godfather of Duke Ernst Ludwig of Pommern´s daughter and had ongoing rapports with Vienna. He was also a very active,

[14] Source: Postcard from 1911 showing the "Reichsgräfl. Schloss".

[15] Together with Heinrich Rantzau.

prolific and diverse man: He regularly donated money to the University of Greifswald to finance poor students; he supported the Duke of Sachsen and Braunschweig in their wars against France and the Turks; he built castles in Löcknitz and Penkun, asked the Italian architect Thaddäus Paglioni to construct a new Renaissance wing for the castle (only partially still existing today), built a church in Löcknitz and helped several villages by implementing a new Lutheran church order. Many clerical figures were amazed by his knowledge and detailed understanding of the bible and different views on dynamics among different confessions. They called him "an expert in Christianity".

When Joachim II died, his son Richard asked artists in Vienna to construct an epitaph out of marble, which can still be seen in the large state church (Landeskirche) in Lieberose (originally it was in the Stiftskirche). It is one of the finest pieces of Renaissance artwork in the old Margrave of Brandenburg.

Picture 9: Epitaph for Joachim II "the Rich" von der Schulenburg (X Generation)

Joachim´s successors lived in splendour and did not manage their estates economically. They lost significant amounts of their land, which could later only be partially offset by a marriage with a rich Countess Dohna in 1609. However, the family was able to retain the estate Lieberose. In 1644 Kaiser Ferdinand III entitled Heinrich Joachim (XIII Generation, 1610-1665) as a "Reichsfreiherr" (a baron who is entitled by the Emperor). Even though

Heinrich Joachim married twice – first a Baronesse Promnitz and later a Countess Solms-Laubach – he remained without children. As he was the last male Schulenburg directly descending from Werner XI, this line died out with him in 1665.

Heinrich Joachim gave Lieberose to his distant cousins from Apenburg who were only allowed to inherit the belongings in case they acquired the "Freiherrenstand"[16], which they did in 1667. Later in the 18th century this part of the family also gained the "Reichsgrafenstand"[17]. As the branch of the family also died out, Lieberose subsequently reached the part of the Black Line family branch named "Tucheim"[18]. Even though the Lieberose family lost significant amounts of their belongings in 1945 when the family´s belongings were confiscated by the Russians, Lieberose was still a business with over eleven thousand hectares of land.

While some branches of the family in the 16th century were evolving toward more "international" careers, others stayed in the Altmark and became successful regional landowners, politicians, trustees, farmers and forest managers.

One notable but sad story in the Schulenburg history took place in the Altmark between the five sons of Levin I (X Generation, died in 1569). Among these brothers, three were very successful and became Governors ("Landeshauptmann") of the Altmark and because of this kept this duty for almost fifty years in the hands of the Schulenburg family. The oldest was Albrecht IV (XI Generation) and he was almost twenty years older than the youngest of the sons named Bernhard. Because of the large age difference, Albrecht took care of his youngest brothers and was a leading figure for his brothers and a whole generation in the Altmark. Albrecht IV[19] became Governor of the Altmark and lived in the Propstei in Salzwedel where he also built the building that still exists today[20].

[16] A title comparable to a Baron.

[17] A „Reichsgraf" is a count that was entitled directly by the Emperor (Kaiser) – it is different from a "reichsunmittelbarer Graf" who had no one between himself and the Emperor (Kaiser).

[18] Later the branch of this family tree died out in 1962 with Count Albrecht.

[19] Georg Schmidt, Das Geschlecht von der Schulenburg, Teil II., pp. 229.

[20] The building was built in 1474. In 1578 the Schulenburgs gave it the structure it still has today. Today the building is used as a museum.

Picture 10: Propstei Salzwedel today[21]

Additionally, Albrecht was the owner of the monastery Dambeck. Part of the occupation as a Governor was to protect the Altmark, keep the streets in good condition, fight crime and robberies, and control and renew "if necessary" the dams in the region.

In 1569 Levin passed away. According to his last will, the five sons were intended to own all the land together. Considering the testament, the brothers were not able to find a fair solution for how to split or own the land in unison, so they entered into a legal fight over the land, which lasted almost five years. In the end they found a compromise shortly after their mother passed away. Everyone seemed to be satisfied with the outcome even though the younger brothers like Bernhard (XI Generation) had to be satisfied with a small house in Salzwedel (Bernhard´s house was located in the Schmiedetraße).

[21] Photo taken in 2002.

Picture 11: Albrecht and his brother Bernhard (XI Generation, both painted in the 16th century)[22]

One night when Bernhard was having a party in his house and invited friends and his brothers, they consumed too much alcohol and argued intensively. When the conflict between Bernhard and Albrecht escalated, Bernhard stabbed his brother Albrecht with a dagger. Albrecht immediately went home to call the doctor. Unexpectedly the experts concluded that the wound was fatal. Albrecht quickly asked for his wife who was not in Salzwedel at the time, so he could still talk to her before he passed away. Fortunately she made it in time to see her husband on his death bed. Albrecht also had asked for the superintendent. Albrecht said with his last breath to the superintendent, "I forgive my brother for his deeds", took the Last Supper and said his last goodbye words to his wife:

"My lovely wife, I would love to be longer with you, if it was god´s will. However, as it may not be that way, please take our destiny with pride and strength. You will not lose me. You are sending me ahead to a place to which you will follow me later".

[22] Source: Photos of the original paintings in 2011.

That night Albrecht IV passed away. His brother Bernhard who had gone to bed after the fight, woke up the next day, claiming he had not planned the attack and that he did not remember most of the night. Even though his brother had forgiven him on his death bed, people recommended him to flee and never return to the Altmark. It was not clear how the family around Albrecht would react and Bernhard´s apology was not believable to most people living in Salzwedel. Bernhard was not a bad man and loved his brother sincerely but he became afraid and left the Altmark. The events of the night and the inner regrets changed his whole life. He travelled aimlessly throughout Europe for five years. After that time far from home, he asked the Duke of Brandenburg to grant him access to his home country again. The Duke gave his permit stating "that it cannot have been on purpose if the suspect goes to bed after his deed and is able to sleep". Bernhard came back to the city of Brandenburg where he lived until the end of his life. He never returned to the Altmark.

Picture 12: Photo in the Audorf church of the altar showing Bernhard asking for forgiveness[23]

[23] Source: Photo taken in the church in Audorf in 1999. Theodore Graf von der Schulenburg (XXIV Generation), to whom this story is dedicated, was baptized in this church on the second Christmas day 2013.

The Thirty Years War: 1618-1648

The Reformation led to a series of religious wars that took place in Europe in the Thirty Years War (1618-1648). The trigger event was the "Prager Fenstersturz" (Defenestration of Prague) in 1618 in which Catholic representatives from the religious Emperor Ferdinand I were thrown out of the window in Prague by Protestants. The war between Catholics and Protestants that started with this Bohemian revolt proceeded to devastate much of Germany over the next thirty years, killing between 25% and 40% of the population. Between 1618 and 1648, the Roman Catholic House of Habsburg and its allies fought against the Protestant Dukes and Princes of Germany, supported at various times by Denmark, Sweden and France. The Habsburgs, who ruled Spain, Austria, Slovene Lands, the Spanish Netherlands and much of Germany and Italy, were staunch defenders of the Roman Catholic Church.

This millennium event also drove the Schulenburgs into poorer and devastating times and left its dark shadows on the family. For example, castle Löcknitz located in Pommern was conquered by Prince Wallenstein (the Emperor's key general during the war), so the Schulenburgs had to vacate the castle. All of the buildings were turned into a fort by Wallenstein. In 1631 the Swedes and the King of Sweden were able to win it back. The Swedes remained at the castle until the "Westfälische Friede" [24] in 1648. By then, the last direct male Schulenburg heir had died and the ownership was given to his daughter and wife. The actual tenure payment connected to Löcknitz (which was extremely high) had to be covered by the remaining male Schulenburgs based in the Altmark (e.g. Salzwedel, Beetzendorf). They were not able to pay it as their savings had also suffered from the long war. Therefore, the family started a legal fight over the lands and the size of the tenure payments. Additionally, there were legal conflicts after thirty years of war had led to ownership changes in the country, which ended in the decision by the Duke of Pommern to confiscate the castle and the land around Löcknitz and turn it into state property. Because of this, one of the nicest and oldest Schulenburg castles was lost to the Duke of Pommern.

Today one can still see in the tower that was built in the 14th and 15th century a sign referring to Joachim II (the Rich) who had built the castle around 1557. The monastery in Dambeck had a similar destiny, as it was ransacked by

[24] The Peace of Westphalia is a term for several peace treaties signed between May and October 1648 in Osnabrück and Münster. These treaties ended the Thirty Years' War (1618–1648) in the Holy Roman Empire. The parties signing had to be in different locations as their rivalry was still too big to speak and negotiate in the same room.

soldiers of the emperor, only to return to the original owner after the Thirty Years War – the Duke of Brandenburg.

Picture 13: Schloss Löcknitz[25]

Other Schulenburg estates were plundered several times and the villages became victims of plagues. Plagues took place several times in Altenhausen, which made the owners flee to the estate Emden for several years. Some Schulenburgs were able to raise only every fifth child they had due to the tough living conditions and diseases throughout Germany. Thankfully it took around three hundred years until the region reached an equally horrible time again.

However, throughout this dark period, one of the most impressive art pieces under the Schulenburgs was created. Oleke von Saldern who was married to a Schulenburg (Albrecht VI, XII Generation), built and decorated the wonderful church of Osterwohle during the Thirty Years War. It can still be visited today and it is one of the most impressive wooden art pieces in Northern Germany from that era.

[25] Postcard showing castle and ruine.

Picture 14: Church in Osterwohle and its wooden interior today[26]

[26] Photo was taken in 2006.

Three Impressive Siblings – Schulenburgs Reaching European Fame and International Presence (17th until 18th Century)

The White Line of the Schulenburgs nowadays has two lines that still exist: The Old White Line and the Young White Line. Other White Lines have died out. The Old White Line goes back to Busso I (VII Generation) who mainly stayed in Beetzendorf and who had successors, including the aforementioned Christoph V or Fritz VIII. Their belongings passed mostly to one person named Friedrich Achaz (XIV Generation, 1647-1701) who lived in Hehlen, Beetzendorf, Angern, Detzel, Osterwohle und Ramstedt. He was married to the beautiful Gertrud von der Schulenburg who came from the Young White Line.

The Young White Line, which goes back to Matthias I (VIII Generation, died in 1477), reached its first peak under Matthias V (XII Generation, 1578-1656) who was a very successful business man active in iron and copper production and a consultant to the King of Sweden. His youngest sons separated the line into Altenhausen (which still exists today) and Emden.

Emden´s head was Gustav Adolph (XIII Generation, 1632-1691) who had many children, among which no male successors. As a consequence, the Emden line died out. Nevertheless, three of the children in the XIV Generation were spectacular figures who made the Schulenburgs reach their peak in history. The oldest sister was the mentioned "Beautiful" Gertrud (XIV Generation, 1659-1697) who married her distant cousin Friedrich Achaz (XIV Generation, 1647-1701) and through this combined the Old and Young White line also for the future. Gertrud´s younger brother Johann-Matthias (XIV Generation, 1661-1747) became one of the greatest generals around the 17th and 18th Century in Europe and was entitled a "Reichsgraf" in 1715 by the Emperor in Vienna. And their younger sister Melusine (XIV Generation, 1667-1743) became the Duchess of Kendal and Munster under George I of Great Britain.

Johann-Matthias – most likely the best-known Schulenburg in history – reached European glory and has been honoured in diverse history books and also in a novel named "The King of Corfu"[27]. He was born in 1661 and his path started quite similar to that of other aristocrats in Northern Germany. He was first raised by a private teacher in his home castle Emden. Afterwards he went to school in Magdeburg, studied for some time in Loire and Paris. His first

[27] Written by Werner von der Schulenburg in 1950.

position was as a "Kammerjunker" for the House of Braunschweig. A Kammerjunker was a job taken by young aristocrats to serve Dukes and Kings to learn and build international relations. Even though being a "Kammerjunker" was a good position for a young person, Johann-Matthias was fascinated by wars and military strategy and quickly left and joined Braunschweig´s and later the Emperor´s armies to start his military career.

Johann-Matthias´ life took place around the Great Turkish Wars, which started in 1683, with a massive invasion force of over 100,000 men marching on Vienna, supported by protestant Hungarian aristocrats rebelling against Habsburg rule. To stop the rebellion and the invasion of Vienna, another alliance was formed. It was composed of Austria and Poland, Venetians and the Russian Empire. These forces fought against the Turks in smaller and larger wars over the next decades, with two milestones – the Treaty of Karlowitz in 1699 and the Treaty of Passarowitz in 1718.

After his position for the Emperor´s armies, Johann-Matthias joined the German regiment and in 1699 he became a Colonel in the service of Victor Amadeus II of Savoy. Two years later in a battle Johann-Matthias was severely wounded. Johann-Matthias´ first steps as a Colonel were not only filled with successes but most of his losses were not considered to be his faults. In 1702 he joined the Saxon Army and fought in the Great Northern War against Charles XII of Sweden. Here Johann-Matthias suffered defeats in the Battle of Klissow and the Battle of Fraustadt. Five years later, in 1707 Johann-Matthias returned to Western Europe and fought under Prince Eugen at the Battle of Oudenaarde and the Battle of Malplaquet in the wars of Spanish Succession. This was a start of a long close relationship between Johann-Matthias and Prince Eugen.

After nine years with the Saxon Army, Johann-Matthias did business in Brandenburg and Mecklenburg over the course of the next few years, met the mathematician and intellectual Gottfried Wilhelm Leibniz in 1714 in Hanover, with whom he had been in written contact for many years, and visited his sister Melusine in London. Throughout his life, Johann-Matthias exchanged correspondence with hundreds of people, including leading politicians, generals, scientists, artists and friends discussing strategies, technology, science and current events, writing in French.

Even though Johann-Matthias wanted to fight for the Imperial military, using all his contacts and close connection to Prince Eugen to set up a deal, Vienna did not offer him the position he was hoping for. However, the army of the

Republic Venetia was looking for a strong and experienced field marshal and general to defend Venetia and their belongings in particular against the Ottoman Turks. He took the position. As a reaction, the Emperor in Vienna made him a "Reichsgraf" and enlarged the Schulenburg crest with additional official decoration. Johann-Matthias had to prepare the Venetian armies to the upcoming war against the Turks.

Picture 15: Johann-Matthias (XIV Generation, 1661-1747)

Johann-Matthias expected the Turks to attack the Venetian island Corfu next. Therefore, he started to recruit troops to the island. From medieval times and throughout the 17th century, the island Corfu was recognised as a bulwark of the European states against the Ottoman Empire. Over time it had become one of the most fortified places in Europe.[28] In a spectacular war over several days, Johann-Matthias was able to defend the island even though the Turks had been able to fight their way onto the island, conquered parts of the fortress

[28] Based on Wikipedia.

and were acting with over sixteen thousand men[29]. In the end the Turks had lost around 8,000 men and the Venetians lost around 1,500 men. Johann-Matthias seized the moment of a weakened Turkish army and struck back against the invading Turks and made them flee. The Turk´s decision to flee was most likely also supported by news about the successes that Johann-Matthias´ ally Prince Eugen of Savoy, together with the Imperial military, were celebrating in the land wars against the Ottomans. Prince Eugene defeated the Turks at Petrovaradin and later he was able to conquer the Banat and its capital Timişoara.

Picture 16: Sculpture of Johann-Matthias in Corfu with the fortress in the back[30]

The following year, after the Austrians captured Belgrade, the Turks wanted peace and in 1718 the Treaty of Passarowitz was signed. The war in Corfu fought by Johann-Matthias until August 1716 was particularly important for Europe as a loss of Corfu would have meant a completely open flank within the European lands and a strategically relevant victory for the Ottomans in Europe. After the war, Johann-Matthias was honoured by all Kings in Western Europe.

---

[29] Dietrich Werner Graf von der Schulenburg, „Geschichte des Geschlechts von der Schulenburg", 1984, p. 160.
[30] Source:
http://commons.wikimedia.org/wiki/File:Est%C3%A0tua_de_Johann_Matthias_von_der_Schulenburg_a_Corf%C3%BA.JPG?uselang=en-gb

A monument for his victory was erected in Venice and in Corfu[31] when he was still alive and he had audiences with the Pope in Rome, received significant awards and remuneration and reached European fame. In 1716 Antonio Vivaldi composed the oratorio "Juditha triumphans" to embrace the victory over the Turks in Corfu and honour Johann-Matthias. Johann-Matthias still lived 31 years after his victory in Venice, was a generous supporter of all of his Schulenburg relatives, and remained as the field marshal and general of Venice until his death in 1747.

As a wealthy person with estates in Northern Germany and Italy and an honourable position in Venice, Johann-Matthias began to become a serious and outstanding art collector starting in 1724. While residing in the Palazzo Loredan on the Grand Canal of Venice, he made his first major purchase when he acquired the 88 paintings by Pierre Puget from a Venetian art-dealer. This collection included works by Raphael, Correggio, Giorgione, Giulio Romano and Castiglione. Many famous artists did portraits of Johann-Matthias, including Bartolomeo Nazari, Giuseppe Nogari, Giacomo Ceruti, Gian Antonio Guardi, Francesco Simonini and Piazzetta. Johann-Matthias worked closely together with the artists and asked them to work on subjects he liked. For example, Francesco Simonini was commissioned to produce paintings commemorating Johann-Matthias´ battles. In Venice, Johann-Matthias supported the painter Guardi with a monthly salary. The famous Canaletto painted for Johann-Matthias a view of Corfu. In addition, Johann-Matthias had access to many royal families, including the Hanoverians, Bourbons, and Habsburgs, and served them as an intermediary host in the Venetian Republic.

[31] Statue by Antonio Corradini who has also made the statue of Karl VI in the National Library in Vienna.

Picture 17: Johann-Matthias´ Palazzo Loredan today[32]

His collected works were transferred in 1736/37 to Berlin to the Palais Schulenburg. Johann-Matthias never married and never had direct descendents. He only had a child from a woman to whom he was not married. His son received the peculiar name "Greifenklau" referring to the Schulenburg crest with the eagle claws. Later they changed the name.

As "Greifenklau" was not a legal descendent, Johann-Matthias gave most of his works to his nephew Adolph Friedrich (XV Generation, 1685-1741), whose mother was the aforementioned "beautiful" Gertrud who had married Friedrich Achaz. The stipulation of the heritage was that the valuable pieces would be kept as a "fideicommissum" (essentially a trust) together in the Palais Schulenburg in Berlin that Adolph Friedrich had built[33].

[32] Source: http://en.wikipedia.org/wiki/File:Palazzo_Loredan_dell%27Ambasciatore_%28Venice%29.jpg.
[33] Source: Dietmar Arnold and Reiner Janick, Neue Reichskanzlei und "Führerbunker": Legenden und Wirklichkeit, page 19.

Picture 18: Palais Schulenburg in Berlin (later Reichskanzlei; destroyed in WWII)[34]

Unfortunately, his will to keep the collection together was not honoured and after his death his collection was dispersed[35]. When Johann-Matthias died, he was first buried in Verona and later taken to Venice where his monument can still be visited today in the Arsenal.

[34] Source: http://commons.wikimedia.org/wiki/File:1895_reichskanzlerpalais.jpg; built in 1736 by Adolph Friedrich in the Wilhelmstraße 77 in Berlin. In 1790 the building was sold to Prince Adrian de Verdy du Vernois. After that it was in ownership of the Duke of Radziwill. After several changes in ownership Bismarck purchased it for the use of the government.

[35] Partially acquired by the King of Prussia, partially auctioned in London in 1775 and partially sold in 1956 by the Schulenburg-Hehlen branch.

Picture 19: Monument for Johann-Matthias in the Arsenal in Venice[36]

Another remarkable life was that of Johann-Matthias´ sister Melusine (XIV Generation, 1667-1743). Melusine was a very thin and tall woman; however, she was not regarded as a beauty. Some Germans named her "the Scarecrow". For this reason, her life path actually surprised a few. She started as "Maid of Honour" to the court in Hanover and the Princess Sophia of Hanover. As Sophia´s husband Prince George Ludwig of Hanover was particularly interested in Melusine, they started a love affair in 1690. In 1694 George divorced Sophia.

With Melusine by his side, George Ludwig succeeded as Elector of Hanover in 1698 and King of Great Britain (as George I) in 1714 and moved to London. Melusine accompanied him. George I "almost certainly" had three daughters with Melusine (even though officially they were held as children of Friedrich Achaz and her sister Gertrud). Melusine had an impressive impact on George I and his policy making. Some people said that she was "as much the queen of England as anyone was." Historians had also remarked the theory that she married George I. This would also be supported by the number of titles that she received by the King – she became the Duchess of Munster, Marchioness of Dungannon, Countess of Dungannon and Baroness Dundalk, in the Peerage of Ireland. Later in 1719 she was further titled as Duchess of Kendal, Countess

[36] Photo taken in 2002.

of Feversham and Baroness Glastonbury, in the Peerage of Great Britain. In 1723, Karl VI, Holy Roman Emperor, created her Princess of Eberstein. "Melusine was able to turn her ambivalent position, an independent aristocratic woman who was at the same time practically the king's consort, to the king's advantage. In 1718 she negotiated with Robert Walpole, then leading the opposition whigs aligned with the Prince, attempting to bring him into the ministerial fold. She also helped George I's existing British ministers, Charles Spencer, third earl of Sunderland, and James, first Earl Stanhope, against the prevailing influence of Baron Andreas Gottlieb von Bernstorff over the king's foreign policy. In persuading George I to allow Sunderland to join the king and Stanhope in Hanover in summer 1719, she gave the British ministers crucial support in their successful bid to exclude Bernstorff from British policy making."[37] She had three daughters. One of them, Petronilla Melusina (1693-1778) married Philip Stanhope, 4th Earl of Chesterfield, who later became a leading Whig politician. As he had no children together with Melusine, he later adopted his godson, a third cousin once removed, also named Philip Stanhope (1755-1815), as heir to the title and estates.

Picture 20: Melusine (XIV Generation, 1667-1743)[38]

[37] Source : http://webcache.googleusercontent.com/search?q=cache:rtGuEqocDToJ:www.oxforddnb.com/view/printable/24834+&cd=2&hl=de&ct=clnk&gl=us&client=firefox-a

[38] Source: http://upload.wikimedia.org/wikipedia/commons/8/8d/Melusina_1.jpg

Prussia under Friedrich Wilhelm I
(reign: 1713-1740)

Living at more or less the same time as Johann-Matthias and Melusine were the nephews, Christian Günther (XV Generation, 1684-1765) and his brother Adolph Friedrich (XV Generation, 1685-1741). They were the sons of Friedrich Achaz and Gertrud and were both raised in Beetzendorf. The two brothers lived very different lives but both benefited from the successes, wealth and fame from Johann-Matthias leading to both of them receiving the "Reichsgrafen" title from Johann-Matthias and being the main heirs – on the one hand there was Christian Günther who lived in glamour, spending a lot of money, and increasing the debt for his estate in Hehlen and on the other hand was Adolph Friedrich who was a tough, educated person having a successful career as an officer for Prussia and trying his best to increase the estates of the Schulenburg family.

Both lived their lives around Friedrich Wilhelm I of Prussia (his father had turned Brandenburg into the Kingdom of Prussia in 1701) who acquired a reputation for his fondness for military display and his strict "Prussian" upbringing and policy. He was known as the Soldier-king (*Soldatenkönig*[39]). Friedrich Wilhelm I wanted his eldest son Friedrich II (Fritz) who was born in 1712 to become a great soldier and brought him up with the strictest military methods. As examples, Fritz was beaten for being thrown off a bolting horse and wearing gloves in cold weather. Unhappy in the world he lived in, Fritz attempted to flee together with his tutor and close friend Hans Hermann von Katte to England, but was discovered. Both of them were brought in front of the court and accused of fleeing from military duties. The highest military judge in Prussia at that time was Achaz Schulenburg from Apenburg (XV Generation "Black Line", 1660-1731). He had become a general under the Soldier-king and was a close ally of Friedrich Wilhelm I.

Pressured by this tough decision, the military court led by Achaz suggested to punish Katte with life imprisonment and declared the decision for the crown-son Fritz a family matter. The father of Fritz, nevertheless, was not satisfied and overruled the war judge (Kriegsgericht) and had Katte executed before the eyes of his son Fritz. Some historians nowadays claim that the King's intention was to also have his son executed. However, this is not clear and in any case the Holy Roman Emperor Charles VI intervened, claiming that a Prince could

[39] His father Friedrich I was able to turn the Margraviate of Brandenburg into the Kingdom of Prussia.

only be tried by the Imperial Diet of the Holy Roman Empire itself. Therefore, Fritz was only imprisoned.

Friedrich Wilhelm I changed the ownership structure of estates of aristocrats in Prussia during these days. Until the first quarter of the 18th Century, the King of a country tenured/endowed his land to a "family" (Geschlecht) for which the larger "family" had to fulfil certain duties to the King. In case a male family "owner" of the land died, the land would be granted to another male family member. The disadvantage of the old system was that the King was able to take away the land from the family in case of misbehaviour or mistreatment which led to conflicts throughout history. The second disadvantage was that the families were not able to sell the land without approval from the King. The advantage of the system was that the land would remain among the male family members and with the Schulenburg name. Additionally, as the King had approved the land to the family it was almost considered as a "holy given" right to stay on the land and to manage and possess it.

The Soldier-king implemented new laws in 1717 that changed the system and made the landlords become direct owners. In exchange they had to pay taxes. However, from then on they were allowed to sell the land without approval. As often the tax payments were even too large for the existing estates, the Schulenburgs were first quite against these new changes but were not able to fight the trend of time. They made contracts among the Houses and lines and tried to manage the old understanding of keeping things in the family and supporting poor family members with "Fideicommiss" contracts.

Independent of the Schulenburgs interaction with the tough young life of Friedrich II and the ownership changes in Prussia, the belongings of the Schulenburgs increased during the 18th century, as the Schulenburgs were very close to the Prussian royal family and had many prominent politicians and officers in their and other regimes (e.g. Levin Friedrich I (XIV Generation, 1675-1729) coming from the House Angern, who was very successful as a General for the Dukes of Savoyen, later the Kings of Sardinia. He acquired the castle and estate Burgscheidungen in the region of the Duke of Anhalt and built the baroque castle complex which still stands today).[40]

[40] After it was confiscated in 1945 it became the GDR CDU party school named after Otto Nuschke, who was the former vice president of the GDR.

Picture 21: Castle Burgscheidungen[41]

[41] Source: http://commons.wikimedia.org/wiki/File:Burgscheidungen_Sammlung_Duncker.jpg; the sculptures in the park are done by Gottfried Jex from Tröbsdorf. The architect was David Schatz from Saxonia. One can still see that the Baroque wings are attached to the old Renaissance wings in the back of the castle.

Prussia's Uprising under Friedrich the Great (reign: 1740-1772)

Coming back to the two sons of Friedrich Achaz and Gertrud – Christian Günther lived during these "Prussian days" a "high life" in and around the court of Hanover. Even though he had been the main heir of the rich uncle Johann-Matthias (who knew the critical situation in Hehlen) and only received his inheritance with the condition that he could only subtract a certain amount of money a year as long as there was debt on Hehlen. Nevertheless, Christian Günther did not follow this condition and his brothers also interestingly did not intervene when he increased the debt amounts in and around Hehlen every year and covered this by decreasing Johann-Matthias´ fortune. When Christian Günther died, his sons were facing such immense liabilities that they could only survive by selling large portions of the inherited estate and the connected belongings. This way and over the next 200 years the Hehlen branch was able to lose one of the biggest fortunes the Schulenburgs had ever created. This is particularly unfortunate as Hehlen is located in Western Germany and therefore would have not been part of the expropriation done by the Russians after the Second World War.

On the other hand, Christian´s brother Adolph Friedrich was able to increase the fortune of the Schulenburgs and was a hard-working individual. He first started his military career for the King of Hanover and later switched to the King of Prussia – the Soldatenkönig – where he quickly moved up the career ladder and spent most of his career. At the age of forty he was General for the Cavalry. When in 1740 the Soldatenkönig died (he did not fight in many battles himself), Adolph Friedrich went to Berlin quickly to congratulate Friedrich II (Fritz, who later became the infamous "Friedrich the Great") for becoming King of Prussia. The young new King was not delighted about his visit and the fact that he had left his regiment just to congratulate him.

Even though Fritz had soon after that given Adolph Friedrich the "Schwarze Adlerorden", which is the highest trophy of Prussia, Adolph Friedrich could tell that his relationship with Fritz was not as good as that with the father Friedrich I. Also, they had different views on strategy and Fritz´ aggressive view of war. This led Adolph Friedrich after many years in the Prussian army to ask Fritz if he could retire. Fritz denied this request and sent Adolph Friedrich into the battle of Mollwitz, which was one of the major battles in the "Erster Schlesienkrieg" between Prussia and Austria.

Picture 22: Adolph Friedrich (XV Generation, 1685-1741)

Adolph Friedrich did not agree that the battle would make sense but followed his leader´s order due to his connection to the Prussian family. Adolph Friedrich died in this battle at the age of 56. His body was carried by his orderly on his horse to Beetzendorf where he was buried under the still existing church in Beetzendorf which he had built a couple of years before in a classicistic style. People say that Friedrich the Great cried when he heard about Adolph Friedrich´s death.

With Adolph Friedrich´s marriage with Anna Adelheid Catharina von Bartensleben (1699-1756) he had gained the impressive estate and castle of Wolfsburg for the Schulenburg family. His oldest son, Gebhard Werner (XVI Generation, 1722-1788), therewith founded the Wolfsburg line of the family.

Picture 23: Castle Wolfsburg today

Because of his creation of this new line, his impressive career as a military officer, his close connections to the two best known Kings of Prussia, his activity as a builder, and his success in increasing the Schulenburg estates, Adolph Friedrich became one of the most important Schulenburgs in the history of the family.

From the French Revolution and the Downfall of The Holy Roman Empire to the March Revolution, the Unification of Germany and the Beginning of the First World War: 1789-1914

In 1789 the French Revolution took place and the Kings of France were removed from power. A decade later, in 1799, Napoleon took over in France and started his wars throughout Europe. In 1806 Napoleon defeated Austria and Prussia and when he entered Berlin, the Governor of Berlin – the successful Prussian officer Friedrich Wilhelm (XVI Generation, 1742-1815) originally from the House of Angern – asked the city to remain calm with his famous saying, "The king has lost his bataille. Calmness is the citizen´s first obligation". Through this, Friedrich Wilhelm was able to save most of the city. In 1806 the Holy Roman Empire came to an end, effectively bringing the era between 962 (when Otto I was crowned as Emperor) and 1806 to an end. This brought a historical shock to Prussian lands and a shift in power that would never again be overcome in history. During these days many Schulenburgs died in the war with France and it took until 1815 for Napoleon to be defeated by the English under Duke of Wellington, and Prussia through Duke Blücher in the battle of Waterloo.

The French Revolution not only had implications for social conflicts between nobility and non-nobility. It was also a driving event for different social matters – among them was the nascent emancipation of women throughout Europe. This can also be seen in the Schulenburg family, when the impressive Charlotte von Friesen, later Countess von der Schulenburg (1798-1874), was born. She wrote a diary about her life, which provides interesting and unique insights into a life of an aristocratic woman of those days. She describes the travesty of the war against the French. Soldiers and civilians died, diseases spread and Charlotte's home village (which was not too far from the battlefields) was home to daily intakes of casualties and wounded people.

After the Battle of Leipzig in 1813, when the coalition armies of Russia, Prussia (at that time led by Gebhard von Blücher), Austria and Sweden defeated the French army of Napoleon, peace started to settle in the lands and normality returned once again.

As a young woman Charlotte describes impressive balls given by Dukes and societies where she became acquainted with the aristocracy of Northern Germany. One day, her sister Louise noticed interest from Charlotte's old friend and distant cousin Werner XXVI Schulenburg (XVIII Generation, 1797-

1829) who was the son of Adolf Friedrich (XVII Generation, 1759-1825) who lived with his family in Dresden as he was head of administration under the Duke of Saxony. This was unexpected for Charlotte, who had interpreted the several dances she had with him as platonic. One night her brother Carl asked her if she would theoretically accept if he asked her to marry him. Even though Charlotte did not have sincere feelings for him, she knew he was an honourable and nice man who was able to give her a very comfortable and safe life. Additionally, her father would appreciate the marriage, so she told Carl that she most likely would accept a potential offer. And so she did. After Werner had asked Charlotte and her father they got engaged and married in 1821/22. Unfortunately for the next years, Charlotte was not able to give birth to a son and she suffered several miscarriages, though she did have a couple of girls. In 1829 the horrible news reached her that her husband Werner had died and she remained a young widow. However, as if by destiny, she was pregnant when Werner died and she gave birth to the desired son named Ernst Friedrich Werner (XIX Generation, 1829-1911) only a few months after the death of her husband. The following years were difficult, since Charlotte had to manage the whole estate by herself at the tender age of 30. Luckily she was able to become the first female guardian for her children in Prussia. She auctioned off smaller parts of the estate that were not necessary, changed lenders that had been taking advantage of her husband and built buildings and an elderly home for employees and agriculture in Beetzendorf. She managed the estate with great dignity and focus, and servants sung her praises. One wrote in a diary "if only the Countess would will herself a bit more sleep" and others praised her impressive results and hard work in and around Beetzendorf.

Charlotte believed strongly in God´s protection and, backed by this belief, she managed the estate and any new task without fear. Several times she travelled to Magdeburg for business and stayed in a hotel where the hosts welcomed her in astonishment, since cholera was pervasive in the city during these days, making it a no man's land for external visitors. Charlotte simply referred to God's protecting hands. Charlotte died at the age of 76 in Beetzendorf after a life of war, cholera, a painful start in her family life, political change in Prussia, and widowhood, though at the same time was able to gain legal independence as one of the first women in Prussia. Following her passing, her only son Ernst Friedrich Werner (XIX Generation) took over the estate and managed it alongside Osterwohle until his death in 1911.

Picture 24: Castle Vitzenburg in 1860 (inherited by Moritz I in 1803 shortly before the French invasion)[42]

The famous March Revolution in 1848 that took place during Charlotte´s days did not impact her life significantly, though it did demonstrate the intellectual upheaval of the time. Throughout Germany there were large popular assemblies and mass demonstrations. They were mainly led by well-educated students and intellectuals. These groups demanded German national unity, freedom of the press, and freedom of assembly. Unlike in other countries where the March Revolution took place, the uprisings in Germany were not well coordinated; however, they had in common a rejection of traditional, autocratic political structures in the 39 independent states of the German Confederation. In the end, the middle-class and working-class components of the Revolution split, and eventually, the conservative aristocracy defeated it, forcing many liberals into exile.[43]

Approximately ten years after the March Revolution with a new Constitution in place for Prussia, Otto von Bismarck – a Prussian statesman – came into power as the Minister President of Prussia (1862-90). He dominated German and European affairs with his conservative policies starting in the 1860s and

[42] Source: http://commons.wikimedia.org/wiki/File:Schloss_Vitzenburg_Sammlung_Duncker.jpg.
[43] Source: Wikipedia Sep-2013.

leading to his dismissal in 1890 by Emperor Wilhelm II. Bismarck provoked wars that made Prussia dominant over Austria and France, and lined up the smaller German states behind Prussia. In 1871, he unified most of the German states (excluding Austria) into a powerful German Empire under Prussian leadership. He then created a balance of power that preserved peace in Europe from 1871 until the beginning of the First World War in 1914.[44]

Born around the time of Charlotte's passing, Bertha (XX Generation, 1861-1940) Schulenburg was another impressive woman living during these times of social change. She had always been interested in women's rights, in the idea of women working and being independent and using Christian values to help socially and in the health field. In 1902 she began as a visiting student at the University of Berlin, studying National Economy. After a couple of years of work in different socially active women groups, she opened in 1909 the "Frauenschule der Inneren Mission" (today's Protestant University (Hochschule) Berlin), where female social workers were educated and where they could take exams and make degrees in different fields. Additionally, in 1909 Bertha had taken a leadership role as a lecturer in the courses "History of Women's Emancipation". She played a significant role in education of women in Germany, especially as she founded in 1917 together with the famous feminist and social work pioneer Alice Salomon (1872-1948) and Anna Weltmann (1881-1947) the "Commission of the Conference of Social Women Schools in Germany". In 1923 Bertha received an honourable PhD (Doctor) in Theology from the University of Berlin. She was one of the first women in Germany to receive an honourable doctor degree. In 1940 she died in Beetzendorf. Her grave can be visited today in the family cemetery.

[44] Source: Wikipedia Sep-2013.

Picture 25: Newspaper article about Bertha Schulenburg (XX Generation, 1861-1940) being part of the women's movement and receiving the honourable doctorate degree[45]

Frauendaheim

Viel Blüten sinken nieder
Im wilden Sturm und Streit. —

Nichts findet sich schwerer wieder
Als Unbefangenheit. F. S.

Weibliche Ehrendoktoren.

Der Wandel der Anschauungen hinsichtlich des Wirkungsgebiets der Frau und ihrer vielfach abgestuften Leistungen gibt sich deutlich zu erkennen in dem Bemühen gelehrter Körperschaften, bei besonderen Gelegenheiten Frauen mit akademischen Gnaden auszuzeichnen. Neben den durch planmäßig vorgeschriebene Universitätsstudien und vorgelegte Dissertationen erteilten Doktortiteln tritt der Doktor honoris causa, der nicht auf Grund einer bestimmten wissenschaftlichen Arbeit erteilt wird, sondern die Bedeutung der Persönlichkeit für die Gesamtkultur ins Auge faßt. Dieses Verfahren, bisher nur an Männern geübt, wird in großzügig vorurteilsfreier Weise nunmehr auch auf Frauen ausgedehnt und trägt vielleicht mehr als die Verleihung des aktiven und passiven Wahlrechts dazu bei, den Gedanken der Gleichberechtigung der Geschlechter in idealer Weise zu fördern. Unschwer läßt sich auch stets die Verbindungslinie aufzeigen, die zu solcher Ehrung geführt hat.

Unmittelbar hat die von der Königsberger ‚Albertina' mit dem Ehrendoktor geschmückte Dichterin Agnes Miegel mit der „Philosophie" nichts zu tun. Aber neben den Weltweisen der aus innerer Nötigung heraus sich die Aufgabe stellt, die mannigfachen Erscheinungen der Welt einheitlich zu denken, tritt von jeher der Dichter, der kraft seiner Phantasie und bildhaften Anschaulichkeit gleichfalls ein Weltbild komponiert. Seit den Tagen der westfälischen Annette ist uns eine solche Fülle balladesker Poesie wie sie in der Miegelschen Lyrik blüht, nicht wieder entgegengetreten. Wir wollen über der genialen Ostpreußin keineswegs die Verdienste anderer großer deutscher Dichterinnen auf gleichem Felde vergessen. Völlig unberechtigt jedoch ist die Frage: warum wird der einen zuteil, was der anderen vorbehalten bleibt? Immer muß man sich vergegenwärtigen, daß solche offiziellen Ehrenbezeigungen Stichproben gleichen, durch die eine ganze Klasse sich herausgehoben und ausgezeichnet halten darf. Als ich zum erstenmal das Rembrandtdunkel der Maria Stuart-Balladen in ihrer wundervollen Kontrastwirkung in mich aufnahm und bald darauf einem größe-[r]en Kreise [...]trug, hatte ich das Gefühl, daß diese Miegelsche Sprache uns neues Schönheitsland erschließen würde. Ähnlich ist es [...] vielen gegangen. Das war in Weimar, als eine Freun[din de]r Dichterin mich auf sie aufmerksam machte, genau um [die sa]mliche Zeit als mich mein Weg zu Frau Elisabeth [Förs]er-Nietzsche, der Schwester des Philosophen, führte, [des]sen zerstreuten und ungesichteten Nachlaß sie die treueste und selbstloseste Hüterin und Bewahrerin geworden ist. Anläßlich ihres fünfundsiebzigsten Geburtstages verlieh die Universität Jena dieser seltenen Frau den philosophischen Doktortitel. Er konnte ihr freilich nichts geben, was sie nicht schon besaß und sich erworben hatte, aber es war eine Promotion, die in den Herzen aller, die Frau Elisabeth Förster persönlich näher getreten waren, freudigste Zustimmung auslöste. Man denke sich diese Frau nur nicht als „atheistischen Freigeist"! Die tiefe christliche Gesinnung, zu der sie sich einst ganz spontan in ihrer Schrift „Neu-Germania" bekannte, ist ihr im Grunde auch heute noch verblieben, denn, ungeachtet ihrer energisch gewollten Hinwendung zu den Gedankengängen des großen Bruders, finden sich in ihren Büchern, in den Einleitungen zu der Taschenausgabe viele Stellen, wo sie bei der Herrlichkeit der Jesusgestalt verweilt, die, ihrer Meinung nach, Nietzsche niemals angetastet habe. Als dieser ihr seine „Morgenröte" überschickte, von der er wohl annehmen durfte, daß sie die christlichen Gefühle der Schwester verletzen konnte, schrieb er dazu: „Lies das Buch unter einem Gesichtspunkt, den ich allen anderen Lesern gerade widerraten würde, aus einem ganz persönlichen Sehwinkel (Schwestern haben zuletzt auch Privilegien). Suche alles heraus, was Dir verrät, was im Grunde Dein Bruder am meisten braucht, am meisten nötig hat, was er will und was er nicht will." Als Nietzsche an dem Druckmanuskript zu „Die fröhliche Wissenschaft" arbeitete, wollte er nicht, daß die Schwester es schriebe, weil er behauptete, ihre zierliche Mädchenhandschrift passe nicht zu dem Inhalt des Buches.

Sie hat sich diese zierlichen aber festen Schriftzüge, in denen sich tatsächlich ihr Menschtum spiegelt, bis ins Alter bewahrt. Zierlich-anmutig und fest, das sind die hervortretenden Merkmale ihres äußeren Wesens, in dem sich umfassende, gediegene Bildung mit hausfraulicher Fürsorge vereinigt. Dieser Dr. phil. hat nicht die meiste Zeit seines Lebens am Schreibtisch und hinter Korrekturbogen verbracht. Der Schicksalsspruch wies zunächst ganz andere Bahnen. In der Führung des brüderlichen Haushalts in Basel, als Kolonisatorin an der Seite des Gatten in Paraguay stählte sich ihre praktische Umsicht zu immer neuen Aufgaben. „Nur wenige Frauen," schreibt ihr der Bruder, „würden mit solcher Tapferkeit, Anspruchslosigkeit und Heiterkeit diese außerordentlichen Schwierigkeiten überwinden. Aber bitte! etwas weniger Bescheidenheit! Vergiß doch nicht, daß die Herde nach pittoresken Menschen verlangt, d. h. nach solchen, die aus ihren Begabungen, Absichten, Erfolgen ein Bild mit so groben,

Bertha Gräfin von der Schulenburg, Leiterin der Sozialen Frauenschule.

Die ostpreußische Dichterin Agnes Miegel.

Elisabeth Förster-Nietzsche, Weimar.

18

[45] Source: http://www.pictokon.net/bilder/05-bilder-2011/1924-10-11-daheim-26-erhrendoktorin-bertha-graefin-von-der-schulenburg-leiterin-soziale-frauenschule.html.

Schulenburgs under the Nazis

After the First World War in which the Schulenburgs lost nine family members and with the fall of the German Monarchy, the Weimar Republic was founded. Between the end of the First World War and the rise of the Nazis, the Schulenburgs were mainly focusing on their own estates and lived a mainly rural live. Some Schulenburgs served in the Reichswehr (later under the Nazis transferred into the Wehrmacht (German Armed Forces)), some were appointed as ambassadors, and still others simply managed their businesses comprising mainly forestry and agriculture. The rise of the Nazis and with that one of the darkest ages in global and German history (and an unparalleled genocide) saw two kinds of responses among the family. Most political parties in Germany that had a reasonable, "moderate" view were weak around 1930, post economic depression. That is why radical groups became more popular among the people. The strongest radical groups in Germany during that time were the very left communists and the far right Nazis. On the one hand, historically the Schulenburgs had been very nationalistic and were interested in a strong Germany. Even though most Schulenburgs did not feel part of either radical side, most Schulenburgs thought that if they had to choose between the two, they would see the Nazis as the better alternative for Germany than the communists. On the other hand, several Schulenburgs recognized the threat posed by the Nazis and did not like the socialist and radical part of the Nazi party (The National Socialist German Workers' Party, or in German, the Nationalsozialistische Deutsche Arbeiterpartei, abbreviated NSDAP, which is commonly known in English as the Nazi Party). They also later were opposed to the injustice brought by the Nazis.

For example, the White Line Schulenburg Friedrich (XX Generation from Tressow, 1865 - 1939) was a very successful official under Emperor Wilhelm´s German army and later became a convinced member of the NSDAP. He became chief of the "Generalstab" of the 6th Army in the First World War. When revolutionary movements took place in 1918 in Germany with the goal of overthrowing the Emperor, the Emperor asked his highest officials to determine whether they should strike against the revolutionists. Friedrich, as a Prussian nationalist, had the opinion that they should try to calm the masses down in the interest of keeping the country together and to be able to have a clear peace negotiation position towards the enemies and to retain the Monarchy. However, Generals Hindenburg and Groener had a different opinion as they believed that the times had changed and the will among the people was too strong. The will of the people for a revolution was just too strong. Times had obviously changed. In November 1918 the Weimar Republic was implemented.

After the war, Friedrich became representative of the German National Party in the Reichstag. In 1931 Friedrich joined the NSDAP, which also demonstrated how much influence Hitler´s promises also had on educated, responsible individuals in Germany. In 1933 – at the same time the NSDAP took power – he joined the SA (German: Sturmabteilung; original paramilitary wing of the Nazis). After 1933 Friedrich was made Representative of the NSDAP in the Reichstag and was selected in 1934 by the SA as a "specialist" for military questions. The same year he left the SA on his own volition and joined the SS (German: Schutzstaffel; a major paramilitary organization under Adolf Hitler) as an "Obergruppenführer". In 1938 he was made General of Cavalry. When he died at the age of 74 years in 1939, Adolf Hitler came for his funeral. Friedrich never saw the start of the brutal Second World War and also did not experience all of the extreme cruelty of the Nazis that took place mainly after 1939 (even though tragic events like the Nürnberger Gesetze or the Kristallnacht did take place before his death).

On the other hand, the Schulenburgs were able to produce two individuals who demonstrated great love for their country, a belief in Christian values including right and wrong and justice, tremendous courage and bravery, and the right contacts and network to become some of the most influential opponents to Hitler in history.

Friedrich´s son Fritz-Dietlof (XXI Generation, 1902-1944) was active as a lawyer of internal administration for the government and other authorities after his studies in Göttingen and his involvement in the fraternity Corps Saxonia Göttingen. Even though hestrongly mistrusted and feared Adolf Hitler, Fritz-Dietlof entered the NSDAP party in 1932. In the years after the takeover by the Nazis, Fritz-Dietlof was disappointed by the unethical policies and injustice practiced and carried out by the Nazis. Fritz-Dietlof was a very nationalistic and conservative character but believed in a just country. As he saw things deteriorate, he looked for people with similar viewpoints and opinions in a different section of the German government. He found several others whom he trusted, had known for some time and who had similar viewpoints. After the war started in 1939, Fritz-Dietlof started to develop thoughts that one would need to depose Adolf Hitler to save the country and end this crime. However, the sweeping success of the German attack on Poland (1939) and afterwards France (1940) made the task of deposing him even more difficult. Subsequently, it became more difficult to find officers with the same mindset. Many Wehrmacht officers who opposed war against the Western powers were proven wrong. Additionally, the war was justified by Germany's revenge against France for the defeat of 1918. Many of these officers supported Hitler's approach, choosing to ignore its darker side.

Nevertheless, several attempts to assassinate Hitler took place also during these early days of the war. Among them was the attempt planned for the 27th of July 1940 in Paris, where Fritz-Dietlof planned to shoot Hitler from the reviewing stand during a military parade. However, Hitler secretly visited Paris in the early hours of the 23rd of July, visiting all of the city's historic buildings on the 23rd from 6am and 9am. After the tour ended, Hitler departed the city. A few days later Fritz-Dietlof received the notice that the military parade originally scheduled on the 27th of July had been cancelled.

In March 1941 at a speech in Posen, Hitler revealed to a select group of army officers his plans for a war against the Soviet Union. Among the audience was the famous Colonel Henning von Tresckow, who had not been involved in any of the earlier plots or attempted assassinations. Nevertheless, he was already a firm opponent of the Nazi regime. He was horrified by Hitler's plan to unleash a new and even more terrible war in the East. Tresckow was well-connected. Assigned to the staff of his uncle's command for a large forthcoming operation against Russia, Tresckow systematically recruited opponents to the group's staff. In this way he made the operation against Russia the new nerve centre of the army resistance and Tresckow and Fritz-Dietlof became more closely connected. As a cover story, Fritz-Dietlof worked for the Ministry of Economics, tough in reality he was working closely together with Henning von Tresckow on the assassination of Adolf Hitler.

Their first assassination attempt against Hitler was planned together in March 1943. Tresckow asked Lieutenant Colonel Heinz Brandt, one of Hitler's staff, to take a parcel with him. It concealed a bomb, disguised in a box with two bottles of liquor. Tresckow's aide, Lieutenant Fabian von Schlabrendorff, set the fuse and handed over the parcel to Heinz Brandt who boarded the same plane together with Hitler. Hitler's airplane was expected to explode about thirty minutes later near Minsk (capital of Belarus), as it was close enough to the front to be attributed to Soviet fighters. General Olbricht planned to use Hitler´s death and the resulting crisis to mobilise his Reserve Army network to seize power. It was an ambitious but credible plan. It might have worked but, as before, luck favoured Hitler. The chemical pencil detonator on the bomb on the plane had been tested many times. It was considered reliable and while it went off, the bomb did not detonate. Due to the unheated cargo hold where the bomb was planted, the percussion cap became too cold and did not explode.

After this unsuccessful attempt, Tresckow and Schulenburg recruited Count Claus von Stauffenberg and modified the Valkyrie plan for a coup against the German government. The modification of the original emergency plan had the intention of using it to take control of German cities, disarm the SS, and arrest the Nazi leadership once Hitler had been assassinated. Fritz-Dietlof was selected to become Interior Minister if the assassination succeeded. On the 20th of July 1944, Claus von Stauffenberg tried to assassinate Hitler under their Valkyre plan but although the bomb in a board room in the "Wolfsschanze" where Hitler sat did explode, the force of the explosion was weakened by a table. When the explosion took place, Fritz-Dietlof was located in the headquarters of the revolt, the military intelligence headquarters in Bendlerstrasse, Berlin.

Picture 26: Fritz-Dietlof (XXI Generation, 1902-1944) and his Family; the photo was taken shortly before the 20th of July 1944

When Fritz-Dietlof heard the news that the attack was unsuccessful and that Stauffenberg had already been shot, witnesses say, Fritz-Dietlof grimly said, "It seems like Germany needs to drink this dreadful glass until it´s empty. We have to sacrifice our lives; people in the future will understand us." He was arrested at the intelligence headquarters the same day, after the attempt on Hitler's life went awry. In August 1944, he was trialled at the notorious Nazi court (Volksgerichtshof). In this show trial, with the infamous Nazi judge Roland

Freisler presiding, Fritz-Dietlof explained his actions with the following statement:

"We took upon ourselves this deed to protect Germany from a nameless misery. It is clear to me that I shall be hanged for it, but I do not rue my deed and hope that another, in a luckier moment, will undertake it."

Fritz-Dietlof was hanged in Berlin-Plötzensee. Only a couple of hours before his end he wrote a goodbye letter to his wife, leaving her behind with five daughters and one son:

"What we have done was insufficient, but in the end history will judge and will release us from our deeds."

Friedrich-Werner (XX Generation from Hehlen and later acquired castle Falkenberg, 1875-1944) was another Schulenburg that was active in the resistance against Hitler, though he had a very different career. Werner joined the German Foreign Ministry after his studies in Lausanne, Munich and Berlin. His career took him to Barcelona, Prague, Warsaw and Tiflis. He served in many different states as a Consul. His first German Ambassadorship was in Persia/Iran from 1922 to 1931 where one can still see an inscription today carved in 1931 into the old stones of the ancient city of Persepolis.

Picture 27: Friedrich-Werner (XX Generation, 1875-1944) inscription at Persepolis in 1931

From 1931 to 1934 he served as the German Ambassador to Romania before being sent to Moscow as the last German Envoy to the Soviet Union before it was invaded by the Nazis. Werner was a specialist in relationships with the East, spoke many languages and was a thoughtful, calm and intellectual character. He was very respected by the Germans and also the Russians. Other employees from the embassy used to describe how Werner twiddled his thumbs when was thinking and stopped to twiddle when he was about to speak – once he did, everyone went quite as they knew he would say something important.

Even though the Nazis´ relationship to Russia worsened year by year, Werner retained a close, personal relationship with Stalin and other Russian senior officials. He was a key person and was highly engaged in the negotiations for the German-Soviet Non-Aggression Pact in 1939, which was one of the key foreign policy accomplishments of the 20th Century history. Unfortunately, the Nazis did not honour the pact, as they did not follow it later when they invaded Russia.

Werner was kept in the dark about Germany's planned invasion of the Soviet Union. He only knew for certain that the invasion would take place a few hours before it was launched. He did, however, get hints of what the Nazis were planning a couple of months before due to a leaked, confidential memorandum. Until the very end, Werner strongly opposed any talk of invasion by referencing Russia´s military strength and the size of their industrial reserves. He even asked for an one-on-one meeting with Hitler, which did take place and lasted around thirty minutes. Werner wanted to speak with him in order to explain the reasons why a war against Russia is disastrous. Hitler did not say anything in the meeting and asked him to go back to Moscow and follow his order. He is quoted as having said to Russia´s Foreign Minister Molotov on the morning of the attack by the Germans:

"For the last six years I have personally tried to do everything I could to encourage friendship between the Soviet Union and Germany. But one cannot stand in the way of destiny."[46]

[46] Source: http://en.wikipedia.org/wiki/Friedrich_Werner_von_der_Schulenburg.

Picture 28: Friedrich-Werner (XX Generation, 1875-1944)

He was a person with courage, which he did not only show in his resistance against Hitler. For example, when the Soviet invasion of Poland took place – despite the ongoing war between Germany and Poland – he used his position as the most senior Ambassador in Moscow to allow Polish diplomats to leave the Soviet Union, when they were being sought out to be arrested by the Soviets.

When the war with Russia started in 1941, Werner was transferred for a few weeks to the Soviet-Turkish border. He was then assigned as Leader of the Russia Committee. This was a foreign ministry position in Berlin with no political influence. However, in Berlin he became closer to Adam von Trott and other people active in the resistance against Hitler. Werner joined the group and later the adapted Valkyre plan under Tresckow. Werner had the opinion that one had to kill Hitler to save Germany. The modified Valkyre plan suggested that Werner[47] would become Foreign Minister after a successful assassination of Hitler. Werner´s first actions would have been to gain peace

[47] Or D. v. Hassel.

treaties with Russia for which he said he would be willing to bypass the German lines in the war. A dialogue about fourteen months before the 20th of July 1944 between Werner and General Felix Steiner went as follows:

Schulenburg: "We lose the war as we are losing breath in the swamp and we are also doing wrong if we do not do anything against it. Hitler is the main reason for the situation. He lets things take place even though he knows about them. That is why he needs to be removed"
General Steiner: "How?"
Schulenburg: "If necessary, with violence"[48]

Unfortunately, after the failed assassination on the 20th July 1944, Werner was captured and as with Fritz-Dietlof, hanged by the Nazis in Berlin-Plötzensee. The videos of him in the trial show that he was already an old man when this took place but his belief in an improved Germany and a clear understanding that injustice has been taking place for many years is still obvious in his answers to the brutal judge Roland Freisler.

In retrospect, the conservative rebels active in the resistance against the Nazis were not only brave, but they also had an astute understanding of right and wrong and a premonition of the horrors to come. They were remarkably forward-looking. A 1943 resistance-group plan for postwar Europe, co-authored by Fritz-Dietlof, says:

"The special thing about the European problem consists of there being, in a comparatively small area, a multiplicity of people who are to live together in a combination of unity and independence. Their unity must be so tight that war will never again be waged between them in future, and Europe's outside interests can be protected jointly...The solution of the European states can only be effected on a federative basis with the European states incorporating themselves into a community of sovereign states by their own free decision."[49]

---

[48] Source: http://www.youtube.com/watch?v=Px2LSEnSdBk.
[49] Source: http://en.wikipedia.org/wiki/Fritz-Dietlof_von_der_Schulenburg.

Schulenburgs after the Second World War – Leaving Homes and Starting a New Life in the West (1945-1989)

In May 1945 the Germans surrendered from a war which had been going on for six years, involving 61 countries and taking over 50 million lives, among them twenty five male and female Schulenburgs. Germany was split into four regions – the French, American, English and Russian areas. The former three built an alliance shortly afterwards. The Russians implemented the communist East named DDR (known to English speakers as the GDR, German Democratic Republic). As both parties wanted to have a stake in the old capital Berlin, which laid like an island in Eastern Germany, the city was split into two parts – a Western and an Eastern part. West Germany named Bonn as their capital as they did not want to have their capital in the East.

In late 1945, a land reform confiscated the land of German aristocrats and of other large land-owners in the East. Additionally, banks were nationalised, an education reform was initialized separating church and state in elementary schools, and heavy industries were nationalized under the guise of confiscation of the property of Nazi war criminals. The land was split into many small pieces and was given to landless farmhands. As most of the Schulenburg estates were located in the East, the Schulenburgs lost almost 90% of their land and had to leave the East with only twenty four hours notice. They were not allowed to bring more than the basic essentials. Because of this, the Schulenburgs, other aristocratic families, and many larger land-owners lost almost all their belongings, treasures and most of their historical pieces. Castles were burned, turned into government buildings, destroyed or just left as they were but without an owner. Treasures, silver, gold, paintings, porcelain, antique furniture and historical weapons were stolen by the government or local people, and thus a large part of the Schulenburg family – but also German history – was destroyed.

The confiscating process also furthered the Schulenburgs´ unhappiness. For example the Wolfsburg branch of the family was already in 1938 forced by the Nazis to sell their castle and land in and around Wolfsburg. The land was considered well located due to its excellent infrastructure based on the East-West water connection on which one could ship coal and metal and the train connections. Therefore, it was foreseen as the prime location for the first Volkswagen plant. With the proceeds of the forced sale to the government, the Wolfsburg family bought new land in Eastern Germany and built a new castle together with the famous architect Paul Bonatz. Unfortunately, the new castle and all the new land (approx. 2,000 hectares out of the total 7,000 hectares estate) were located in Eastern Germany and were therefore lost to the Communists in the DDR a couple of years later.

Picture 29: Castle Neumühle today

The Wolfsburg branch was not the only Schulenburg line to be hit by DDR´s policy. Among other estates, the Schulenburgs lost due to the communist policy in the DDR and Poland Filehne with over 12,000 hectares[50], the wonderful castle of Beetzendorf (black and white line) with many townhouses and over 4,600 hectares, the beautiful castle of Lodersleben, the estate and castle around Burgscheidungen[51], the castle of Emden, Altenhausen with over 1,500 hectares and many historical treasures and artefacts.

As an embodiment of the difficulties of this time, Rosemarie Schulenburg (1920-today, born "von Blücher") has captured her remarkable and harrowing life in her autobiography, "What my grandchildren wanted to know". Rosemarie came from Wolkow which is a small village in today's Poland. Before she received her high school degree she had to switch schools three times, because the schools were closed as Non-Nazi Schools. After school she was sent to occupied Poland as a social worker (Arbeitsdienst) where she saw with her own eyes the Nazi crimes that took place. She always dreamed of studying medicine which she was only able to do for a few years at the

[50] Today Polish land.

[51] However, this was lost shortly prior to the confiscation by the Russians, as the Fideikomiss rule was no longer allowed and the last owner had no son.

University of Marburg. As a student she joined the anti-Nazi movement of the catholic student church community. She had to abandon her studies when she married Werner Schulenburg (XXI Generation, 1908-1979) from Beetzendorf in 1943, because she had to manage the estate Beetzendorf owned by her husband who was sent to war. Werner belonged as an officer to the military government in Belgium, which was part of the planned assassination of Hitler on 20th July 1944. After the 20th of July 1944 the military government was dissolved and he was sent as a punishment to the Russian front where he was severely wounded in the first days. In Beetzendorf, Rosemarie endured occupation, expropriation, and house arrest by the Russians. Following a miraculous rescue, she escaped with Werner to the West without having anything and had to start a new life, forced to abandon their family home for the last 700 years. Werner, who had been raised as a wealthy man from the estate Beetzendorf, decided after the war and all his personal experiences in Russia to become a pastor in the Lutheran church, once they moved to Western Germany. He believed that Germany would only find its way back from "pseudo-religion of National Socialism" by turning to its Christian roots.

As only a few remaining Schulenburgs still owned their estates or significant belongings after World War II, most Schulenburgs started new and different careers as businessmen, researchers, teachers, officers in the new army, professionals such as lawyers, medical doctors, artists, civil servants, and diplomats. Some Schulenburgs left the country and moved to the United States, South America, the UK or elsewhere. The Schulenburgs moved toward modernity and adapted to the new situation of the family and its individuals. Some of them did very well and succeeded in developing small fortunes again, participated in international politics, became renowned researchers or contributed to scholarship or culture as narrators or famous photographers. Despite the huge fall of the family, they were able to lead their way to the modern world.

When in 1990 the unification of Germany took place, old landowners that had been forced to leave did not get their land back but received a "pre-emption right" to repurchase small portions of their old estates. If they did not use the pre-emption right, the estate was auctioned. At present, over ten Schulenburgs opted for this right and have reacquired old estates with forestry and agriculture. Additionally, some of these families reacquired Schulenburg castles in Eastern Germany and consequently went back to their old homes. Most of the funds needed to acquire these estates were made in normal jobs or by starting smaller businesses in Western Germany. This return to the old roots has been done by several Schulenburg members; Hubertus (XXI

Generation, 1943-today) acquired parts of the forest around Altenhausen[52]; Johann-Matthias (XXII Generation, 1950-today) purchased parts of White Line Beetzendorf and the old forestry home Groß Wismar; Günther (XXIII Generation, 1965-today) expanded the Wolfsburg line estate by acquiring forests around castle Neumühle; Paul-Werner (XXI Generation, 1936-today) bought agricultural land in and around Apenburg; Werner (XXII Generation, 1944-today) acquired parts of the forest in Lieberose; and Alexander (XXII Generation, 1968-today) purchased the castle and the forest in Angern. Alvo (XXII Generation, 1939-today) bought the forest in Schricke and Hardnak (XXI Generation, 1934-today) purchased Trampe with the agricultural land and forest.

Picture 30: Castle Altenhausen today[53]

Today the Schulenburgs look back at a history of over 777 years with 24 generations. Every male Schulenburg can be traced back to Werner, who was first documented in 1237. There are over fifty living adult male family

[52] The castle has been turned into a hotel hosting weddings and other events.

[53] Source: http://commons.wikimedia.org/wiki/File:Altenhausen,_Schloss.jpg.

members and over one hundred members in the larger family. The current head of the family is Johann-Matthias (XXII Generation, 1950-today) from the "White Line" of the Beetzendorf branch. As an old tradition, the family still meets every two years for a family gathering, which allows them to see each other in different places throughout Germany and Europe, to keep in touch and to discuss their history, current events, changes in the family and plans for the future.

Picture 31: Family Gathering in Wolfsburg in 2011

Appendix 1: Map

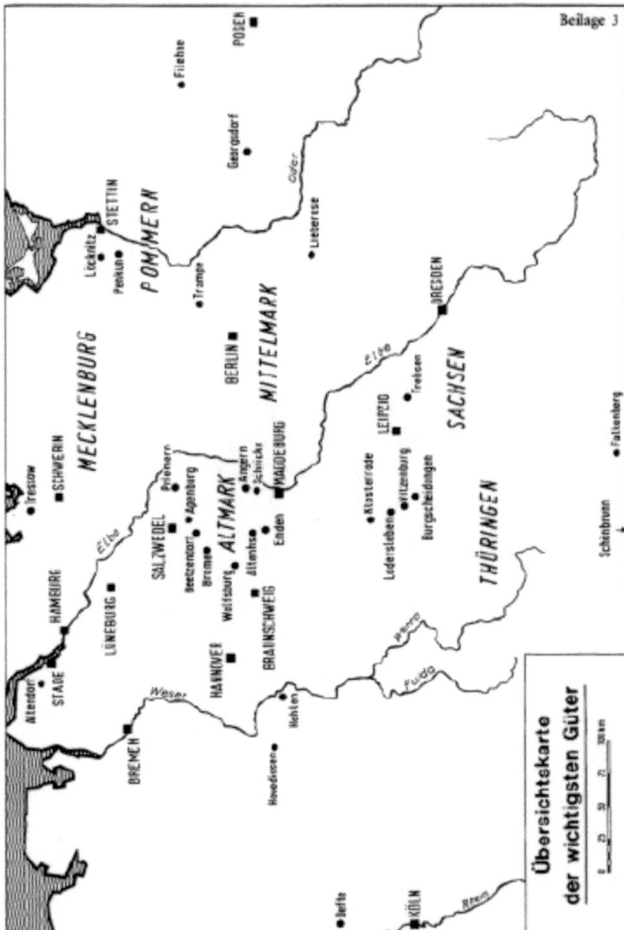

Source: Werner Graf von der Schulenburg, „Geschichte des Geschlechts von der Schulenburg", 1984.

Appendix 2: Overview of Mentioned Schulenburgs

Generation	Name	Comments
I	Conradus	Signed treaty (1187, only a copy from the 16th century exists today)
II	Wernerus	Signed first remaining treaty mentioning a Schulenburg (1237)
III	Werner II	Endowed with the castle close to Salzwedel and father of Bernhard I and Dietrich II, 1271-1304
IV	Bernhard I Dietrich II	Formed the White Line (1340) Formed the Black Line (1340)
V	Dietrich III	Bishop of Brandenburg (1365)
VI	Bernhard VI	Minister of Salzwedel (1416), 1406-1453
VII	Busso I	Born around 1396
VIII	Werner XI Matthias I	Key figure around the "Prenzlauer Frieden", +1515 Governor of Altmark, +1477
IX	Richard II	Bought 1519 Lieberose, + 1536
X	Georg V Joachim II Levin I	1513-1560 "Joachim the Rich", 1522-1594 Governor of Altmark, father of five sons, 1510-1569
XI	Richard III Christoph V Fritz VIII *Ilse von Saldern* Matthias III Albrecht IV Bernhard XIII	Son of "Joachim the Rich", 1547-1600 Bishop of Ratzeburg, 1513-1580 Bought Hehlen (1560), 1518-1589 *Married to Fritz VIII, built castle in Hehlen, 1539-1607* Supporter of Martin Luther, 1506-1542 Governor of Altmark, 1535-1583 Killed his brother Albrecht IV (1583), 1557-1601
XII	Albrecht VI *Oleke von Saldern* Matthias V	1557-1607 *Married to Albrecht VI, built church in Osterwohle, +1622* 1578-1656
XIII	Heinrich Joachim Gustav Adolph	1610-1665 Father of Johann-Matthias, Melusine and Gertrud, 1632-1691
XIV	Friedrich Achaz Gertrud Johann-Matthias Melusine Levin Friedrich I	Married to his cousin Gertrud, 1647-1701 Married to her cousin Friedrich Achaz, 1632-1691 Defeated the Turks in Korfu (1716), 1661-1747 Duchess of Kendal and Munster under Georg I of Hanover, 1667-1743 General for the Dukes of Savoyen, built Burgscheidungen, 1698-1729
XV	Christian Günther Adolph Friedrich *Anna von Bartensleben* Achaz V	Inherited Johann-Matthias´ art collection and Hehlen, 1684-1765 General under Friedrich I and II of Prussia, 1685-1741 *Wife of Adolph Friedrich, contributed Wolfsburg, 1699-1756* Judge over Hans Hermann von Katte and Friedrich II (1730), 1660-1731
XVI	Gebhard Werner	Founder of Wolfsburg branch, 1722-1788
XVII	Adolf Friedrich	Head of administration under the Duke of Saxony, 1759-1825
XVIII	Werner XXVI *Charlotte von Friesen*	1797-1829 *Managed Beetzendorf, founded hospitals and institutions, 1798-1874*
XIX	Ernst Friedrich Werner	1829-1911
XX	Bertha Friedrich Friedrich-Werner	Founder of the "Frauenschule der Inneren Mission", 1861-1940 General of Cavalry, 1865-1939 German Diplomat and part of resistance against Hitler, 1875-1944
XXI	Fritz-Dietlof Friedrich A. Werner *Rosemarie von Blücher* Hubertus Paul-Werner Hardnak Alvo	Part of resistance against Hitler, 1902-1945 Director of Johanneswerk in Bielefeld, Head of the Family, 1908-1979 *Author of "What my grandchildren wanted to know", *1920* *1943 Head of the Family, *1936 *1934 *1939
XXII	Johann-Matthias Werner Alexander	Head of the Family, *1950 *1944 *1968
XXIII	Günther J.-Friedrich (Fritz)	*1965 *1985
XXIV	Theodore	*2013

Short Background on the Author:

Graf Johann-Friedrich (Fritz) von der Schulenburg-Beetzendorf was born in Berlin (Germany) in 1985. As a scholar of the Studienstiftung des Deutschen Volkes, Fritz studied economics and art history at the University of Vienna and the London School of Economics and Political Science. Fritz is particularly interested in history and art and has occasionally appeared as a curator of contemporary art exhibitions. Today, Fritz lives and works in Frankfurt am Main where he is active in the Private Equity industry.